In Memory of Theresa Cleary

For Phyllis

15 June 06
Poetry
Shelter Island *$6-*
12/23

Looking for
the Uncertain Past

Daniel Thomas Moran

Foreword by
Daniela Gioseffi

with my admiration

POETRY SALZBURG
at the University of Salzburg

SALZBURG

2006

First published in 2006 by **POETRY SALZBURG** at the University of Salzburg

EDITOR: WOLFGANG GÖRTSCHACHER
EDITORIAL ASSISTANT: ANDREAS SCHACHERMAYR

ISBN: 3-901993-24-X

INSTITUT FÜR ANGLISTIK UND AMERIKANISTIK
UNIVERSITÄT SALZBURG
AKADEMIESTR. 24
A-5020 SALZBURG
AUSTRIA

http://www.poetrysalzburg.com
editor@poetrysalzburg.com

Contents

Acknowledgements

Thanks are due to the editors of the following magazines where some of these poems have previously appeared:

Artaction, Asinine Poetry, Confrontation, Humanist Living, Journal of the American Medical Association (JAMA), Long Island Pulse Magazine, LSR, Nassau Review, Newsday, Northport Arts Magazine, Pedestal Magazine, Poetry Salzburg Review, Prairie Poetry, Rattapallax, The Seventh Quarry, The Shelter Island Reporter.

An American Poet Ready for the New Millennium

Looking for the Uncertain Past is a collection of poems that shows Daniel Thomas Moran, Poet Laureate of Suffolk County, New York, to be a writer very much in the modern American, William Carlos Williams tradition. His poetry is appealing and pleasurable, not laborious, to read. It is accessible in its ironies and profundities and very much concerned with close observance of everyday life. William Carlos Williams was a physician and a poet who, according to many literary critics and scholars, changed the face of American poetry for generations to come and influenced it for the better. Williams wedded the divergent styles of the two most internationally known icons of nineteenth-century American poetry: Walt Whitman and Emily Dickinson. We are reminded that neither of these greatest of American poets wrote their works from "halls of ivy". Using Whitman's natural cadence with Dickinson's economic, and sometimes sardonic, lyricism – Moran, like Williams, writes in an American idiom in touch with actual everyday life. He does not look down from a rarified, ivory tower, as do many academic poets of our time, but from the vantage point of a scientist connected to reality.

> Writing a poem
> is not like
>
> rising at first light
> to cook for an army,
>
> but more like
> waking at ten on Sunday
>
> to prepare an omelet
> for someone you really love,
>
> or teaching a small child
> to lace up a shoe.

("At Hard Labor", p. 85)

Like Williams, in his often quoted poem, "The Red Wheelbarrow", the deceptively simple truths Moran sets down for us have much larger implications. As the poet never loses his hold on the real world, his poetry rises unaffectedly out of the natural sphere. So much so that his craft is seamless with his observation. Sometimes, as in "One Moment along a Street in Kensington", it is made all of artful description in observations of ordinary moments that the writer raises into the realm of poetic vision by making us look closely and carefully at common-place moments peopled with ordinary people.

> Behind window glass,
> cut into a recess of brick,
> and four floors over the street,
> the lady of the house is standing,
> [...]
>
> Rain clouds
> withhold and somersault
> over the rooftops.
>
> Behind the window
> the lady guides water
> over a breakfast dish,
> lays down the rag
> to scratch at
> a reluctant speck
> of clotted egg.
>
> [...]
> The taxi is lost
> along the distance
> as is the next.
>
> The lady of the house
> disappears into
> the silent inner elsewhere,
> as the last of the moisture
> runs from the plates,
> [...]
>
> ("One Moment along a Street in Kensington", p. 102-103)

In the tradition of Williams mentioned above, note how the mood is established and we realize life is composed of small happenings, the viscera of washing dishes observed through a window, simple labors of the body that sustain us and therefore bring peace to the hungry spirit.

Perhaps being a doctor of dentistry in close contact with patients – quite literally looking life in the mouth – has made Moran a poet of reality, not mere mental machination. He is an intellect who labors with his hands, touching real life, viewing the tongue that makes language in its daily dance of articulation. It is the tongue against the gums and teeth that articulates experience, which tastes with the mind in unison with nerves leaping over their synapses to afford feelings of being alive. Seeing, touching, hearing, tasting, smelling is what life is about. Without the reality of the senses there is no life.

Yet, as in Rabelais, there is often, also, philosophical humor in these poems.

Faith

Is the Act
Of Throwing
Seeds into an
Ocean, believing there
Will be a Garden when
One Returns.
                    ("Catechism", p. 33)

Moran's poetry talks with sardonic wit and sensitive spirit without sending us puzzling away from its lively clarities. A sharp intellect is also at work in these writings, an eye for absurdity as well as for the splendors in the everyday.

Regret is the
great venom,
the path not
chosen finds
only the lost.

[…]

Just as death
lives in the
shadows left
behind, the day's

fruits will
lie wilted by
a sun which
made them sweet.

("Opus 75", p. 73)

In a July 31st, 2005 article by Julia C. Mead, in *The New York Times*, Moran is quoted as saying he feels himself to be part of a Long Island School of Poetry, inspired by Walt Whitman. Whitman was born of Paumanok, a land mass surrounded by the sea but very near the giant cosmopolitan City of New York. With fellow Long Island poet and professional fisherman, Allen Planz, Moran argues that the Long Island School of Poetry is one of place, steeped in the lore and lure of island light and ocean's roar, as well as the intimacy of direct address fostered by Whitman. In "A Former Son of the Beach", Moran writes: "Oh, there were years I would long for the sea, / Sleep to the sounds of it pounding the shore. [...] // As a child I looked out across it with wonder, [...]." (p. 46) Long Island's Suffolk County poets are also poets of the great metropolis, the nearby international culture of the City of New York which also permeates their poems.

Though much of Moran's poetry arises from Long Island's shores, he is cosmopolitan, in this collection, and in his others, as well. His poems take us from New York to Prague, from Paris to Kensington or Venice, from Salzburg to Minnesota. He returns to his Italian as well as his Irish ancestry. In "From Farnan's Well", Moran writes: "I've been down to Ballymeeny, / to speak with the wind / and the dead," (p. 22) but, much of his spirit believes in "Staying Put", on the whale-shaped island that juts out from New York City's shores into the Atlantic where the poet has edited a collection of Suffolk County poets. Moran lives between the flukes of Long Island's tale on Shelter Island, an island nestled within an island, from which he writes:

There is a field very near Easthampton,
and just along Stephen Hand's Path
where yesterday and today, the rye grass
lies wilted by ice, gold like the dappled golds
van Gogh laid down with his stiffest broadest brush.

Across its soft arc, scattered like ladies at a lawn party,
an uncountable number of Canada Geese,

[12]

[…]

They have no more desire for the fabled flights in chevron,
[…]
Settled on this spit of earth, between Ocean and Sound,
they have embraced the middle, content to go nowhere.

("Staying Put", p. 25)

Moran knows the struggles and contradictions of his Irish and Italian immigrant ancestors, and their Old World beliefs. He has rejected their forms of superstition to embrace a New World rhymed by reason that can lift us from despair as we observe with objectivity and humor the jazzy cacophony of an American landscape. We can laugh at ancient Abraham's legendary predicament, and reject a murderous and sacrificial God to embrace a "Beat" generation's vision of reality, one that offers a Romantic will for imagination. Like his contemporaneous generation of poets, who took their term "Beat" from the word "beatific", as much as from the improvisational, rhythm of American jazz, Moran's observations also travel through the funky alleys and beautiful byways of everyday capturing the essence of "tin men and popes" – noting everything on the scene, or in the news, from "sharks to Elvis", Secretary of State Condolezza Rice to the C.I.A, to the heart rending plight of children of Darfur,

At Darfur,
the children, weak
from emptiness,
accord the flies
the tears
from their eyes.

("On Compassion", p. 75)

And, like Ralph Waldo Emerson and Nathaniel Hawthorne, two seminal American Transcendentalists, he scolds those who spend too much time dwelling in the darkness of superstition and scriptural hypocrisy – instead of in human realms of *possibility*, where knowledge of reality can lift us to the sublime, and make us humane, here and now, on the natural earth. In that sense Moran offers a moral guide for our conscience and asks us to pay attention to what is real. His poetry seems to tell us that knowledge of that which is actual, science and truth, visited by imagination, creates cures for human suffering. His writing reveals a very likeable guy with his feet on the ground and his head in what Dickinson called "possibility" her word for "poetry" and "imagination". Like Whitman, Moran "sings the body electric" its joy in sensual pleasures. He realizes our biology, our life force, as well as our ability to dream the impossible even as we are bound by mortality. As in Dickinson and Whitman, the force of love as an emotion is the redeemer of hope and the harbinger of pleasure.

> The day will be upon us soon
> When I will need to raise up
> My face to see into your eyes,
> When I will need to be
> Reassured by your shoulders.
> Someday I will need to
> Call out to you to come close
> And make of your hands
> A cradle for my head.
>
> ("To My Young Son", p. 54)

> […] the rain
> is ferocious tonight.
>
> So much that I fear
> the hills will be washed away.
>
> And if I am not mistaken,
> there may be someone
>
> at my door.
>
> ("At Hard Labor", p. 86)

Moran's poems proceed naturally without contrivance, and the ironies pointed out often strike us as witty afterthoughts. Yet, we catch our breath and grieve or laugh with the poet in unison with his compassionate humor. His writing is both sensitive and muscular and divulges the mind of a rational observer who does not miss nuance and cannot be fooled by artifice. His virtuosity is so natural that it does not take us away with the music, but keeps us in the thought, as Emerson advises in "The Poet", 1841, an essay quite influential upon the work of both Whitman and Dickinson in forging a very American poetry:

For it is not meters, but a meter-making argument that makes a poem – a thought so passionate and alive, that, like the spirit of a plant or an animal, it has an architecture all it's own, and adorns nature with a new thing. The thought and the form are equal in the order of time, but in the order of genius the thought is prior to the form.

Moran sees the world in a grain of sand. His poems often begin with acute observations of people, places, and things, then establish a mood, and finally crystallize a vital truth – often with a sardonic smile. And that word "sardonic", not "satiric", is the word, as satire can be cruel and sets the author of the mockery apart from us. Moran lives among us, not above us, and draws us into laughing at ourselves rather than mocking us from some high perch.

> If I try, I can see things your way.
> You know I want to, but
> it feels like I'm forcing my foot
> into a shoe which is ill-fitted.
> [...]
> After all, we are all humans,
> each of our skulls slightly misshapen,
> and filled with such separate thoughts,
> each of us fighting back the overgrowth
> along the course of our chosen path.
> [...]
> We can agree that it's only fair, then
> having given both opinions fair chance,
> at least one of us will be certain,
> that you were completely wrong.
>
> ("To the Woman at the Party Last Night
> Who Just Had to Bring It Up", p. 104)

Though Moran portrays folly with temperate drollness, he can sometimes bite:

> Even when my Grandmother
> was without her apron,
> it was hung in plain sight.
> Married sixty-two years
> to a man who had her spend
> the long Upstate Winters,
> blanching and jarring tomatoes

[15]

he had grown from specks.
[...]
She pulled at the stones with
the teeth of a rake, to make
room for the fruits to breathe.
In his angry old age,
he would berate her while
she rinsed the greasy sauce
from his dinner plate,
concerned she was wasting soap.

("The Queen of Carolina", p. 44)

Moran is a very American poet with an Irish twinkle in his eye and an Italian sense of the tragic. He does not set himself apart from the ironies of life, but lives them with us, not mocking our frailties, but simply sharing the plight of our human paradox. He knows our sadness and frailty, but insists on hope as the element that keeps us lively at the heart of love and longing.

This morning, I left our bed early.
You know how, with the early sun and silence,
my mind begins to spin like that mysterious machine
at the carnival which makes cotton candy.
I try not to disturb you, but I imagine you alone,
wandering in some storied forest with only
the lights of a big moon to suggest your steps.
[...]

This morning, I am in your chair, playing out
all the many cards of my life. The air, the piano
and our cats are all still and I am listening, as I do
for you to call out in your sleepy voice and let me know
that you have returned.

("Saturday or Sunday Morning, Early", p. 48)

Some of Moran's poems brood and mourn our common fate: "We must begin / by loving the dust, / for it is indeed / everywhere in this world." ("Al Qaeda Training Films, Inc.", p. 40) Or, "In this world, / orphans beget orphans. // Misery throbs" ("Orphans", p. 26) but, always his eyes are open to absurdity and contradiction, a sense of humor that sustains and comforts. We have to laugh at ourselves, because our lives are finite and we are ultimately mortal, no matter

[16]

how high our endeavors reach. Love is always the redeemer of all, as there is no god but love in Moran's universe. Love is *the force* that saves us from our folly and our misery. Love *is* God, and there is no other god before the force of human love itself, for Moran is ultimately a Humanist in the best sense of the word. He calls upon us to be kind to one another, here and now, without any dreams of a heaven beyond this glorious earthly realm, the paradise that is here on earth if only we will live deeply in it, feeling, touching, tasting, seeing, hearing the splendor that is real and not a mere dream of peace and beauty beyond our grasp.

> Two squirrels
> chase the last
> hours of autumn
> through a mantle
> of brittle leaves.
> [...]
>
> Tonight
> a warm touch
> will be welcome.
> [...]
> And perhaps
> a single
> green thought
> of spring.

("To Begin Winter", p. 52)

Because Moran sees the glory in everyday being, he has no wish to reach beyond life for fulfillment except in leaving it to the next generations to come. Thus of all things, he wishes a child for his son, as in "On Your Fourteenth Birthday". That stance of hoping for a child for his child creates a responsible human, here and now, and makes the poet reluctant to leave this lovely earthly realm with all its contradictions. He does not pretend that death brings rewards.

> When my time comes.
> Don't lay me in a box
> with long bronze handles.
> Don't comb my hair
> the way you always

thought it should go
and lay my head on satin.
[…]
And please no churches,
no suggestions of the
mysterious will of
a god I deny.
[…]
Be certain that
I did not go willingly. Yet,
[…]
I will not raise up
a single objection, only
be sure to have someone
say that given the chance,

I would have stayed a bit longer.

("Some Instructions", p. 112)

Looking for the Uncertain Past is a pleasurable collection to read, because it affords an ease of intimacy with the poet, sharing the everyday irony, fun and sadness, pleasure and pain of being. In the American tradition of poets, these poems offer the naturalness of Whitman's diction, wed with the economy of Dickinson's lyricism. Moran's poems speak of a poetic awe of reality, informed by intelligent observation. He brings together two very different transcendental styles of American writing. Like Williams, he unites them by meshing the best of both. These penetrating poems – deceptively simple – celebrate, narrate, elegize, and eulogize bringing surprising insights with precise, but everyday language, and occasionally with Chaucerian humor that rises to hilarity. They are both elegant and accessible and refresh the spirit with enjoyable contemplation.

Daniela Gioseffi, New York City, 2006

LOOKING FOR
THE UNCERTAIN PAST

To Karen before a Storm

I am wishing for
a thunderstorm tonight,
one which will come
from the slow distance,
silhouette our trees in
winks of dim light,
shudder them with echoes.

We will be waiting,
you and I.

Composed as two notes
hung in the electric air,

watching the night
without blinking.

And it should
build like Brahms,
causing us to slowly
close the hollows
between our hands.
It should burst
all the quiet,
teach us how

life can
begin and end,

in the space
between heartbeats …

From Farnan's Well

for Yvonne Henry

I've been down to Ballymeeny,
to speak with the wind
              and the dead,
beside a
      smooth swale of shore
which slid like a penstroke
     away   from Ben Bulben.
I stood,
            at the top of a lane,
               rutted by rain
and a farmer's wood wheels,
humbled
by a horizon
       which birthed our days.
Against
    a sky of rare cyan,
the clouds tumbled like
        cream   into   tea.
I looked
          to the glen where
your freshet fell from
            the hills.
I looked
     for you, Delia Kilcullen,
filling your bucket at
      Farnan's Well,
your feet,   like mine,
     wet with this mud.
I looked for
        your brothers, and your
Father calling for
the strayed lamb, and your
Mother feeding
       turf to the fire.
They were all

                    so young, and you
but a girl when you left them,
                wild and unsettled
as the briar among these
                    well-placed stones.
A girl who knew not far
            beyond this darkened door,
lived all the stars which
ever were.
You slept dreaming to the
                    whispers of waters
never stilled,   and with
your bucket at each aurora, you
imagined the sun lifting the sea,
                from the Sligo hills.

To Begin a New York Day

At The Westside Diner
breakfast arrives
as he likes it.
Eggs barely over.
Hash Browns and Links.
Rye toast light.

Downtown,
the early bird
from Logan
pierces the
North Tower
as he

splits his yolks
and lays the
ketchup on thick.
On the front page,
stocks are up,
crime is down.

The first red truck
flies by on Columbus.
The waiter he
always calls George
tops off his cup
with decaf.

As the
first tower falls,
he folds *The Times*
as best as he can
and raises his hand
for the check.

Staying Put

There is a field very near Easthampton,
and just along Stephen Hand's Path,
where yesterday and today, the rye grass
lies wilted by ice, gold like the dappled golds
van Gogh laid down with his stiffest broadest brush.

Across its soft arc, scattered like ladies at a lawn party,
an uncountable number of Canada Geese,
babies lost now in that vast crowding.
A million footprints in the snow,
more swarm than flock, in a slowed motion of sepia tones.

They have no more desire for the fabled flights in chevron,
palm trees in Winter and Summer in a cool northern pond.
They have abandoned Canada and the miracle of migration.
Settled on this spit of earth, between Ocean and Sound,
they have embraced the middle, content to go nowhere.

Orphans

In this world
orphans beget orphans.

Misery throbs
like a distant drum.

If only agony
were bread and
despair a cool stream.

If only futility
were wisdom and
anguish a field
of sunflowers
stretching toward
the copper plum
horizon.

We wonder, Where
do they come from,
these children who are
joined at the head?
Eyes fixed
upon their ceilings.
A wide part in their hair.
Unable to see what
is holding them back,
they struggle
to make the first move.
They are too young
to know, it's not what
any mother could intend,
aiming high for
grace and for speed,
for long lives filled
with moments of solitude
to reflect upon miracles.

JOINED AT
THE HEAD

Who could imagine
that things could go
so very wrong?
Yet, we look on
in troubled amazement.
We lie awake
alone at night, or not.
And if we can be wise
and recognize ourselves
even when others are
uncertain who is who,
Remain free of
all constant reminders.
We must say to us,
even alone
on a crowded street,
that all entanglements considered,
it could have been worse.

In Memory of Willi Braunschweig

† February 2004

It is barely
Tuesday, and you
are already ash,
consumed in that
fire which bridges
this world and the next.
The last of your lines
have settled high
among the balcony seats.
Your size not stature.
Faces assumed
became footnotes
against the footlights.
You knew so well
it was all only acting.
You shaped the words
with both hands
until life became
larger than itself.

A space has been emptied.

But we shall
still hear that voice,
caught between
the sound of wind
through maples
and the creak of
an old porch chair
left out all winter.
We are left with a
curl of pale smoke
off the glowing
of a long cigarette,
and the crown of

that great straw hat
which you would
tip to the fore and
lower like a sunset
between a smile and
your most gentle bow.

In die Ferne radeln wir*

The German cyclists
ride in tandem,
forward facing,
heads and limbs
of pressed tin,
four feet
pinned to pedals.
Their sprockets
chained
one to the other,
shirts speckled
red on yellow.
Their bicycle, blue
as the Danube,
contains the
simplest of springs;
a ribbon of steel
wound around itself.
Weight over
white rubber wheels,
they travel only
in the tiniest circles.
On our sill
they lean into
an imagined headwind,
a thought
with four legs,
and contemplate
the distant.

* Into the Distance We Are Cycling

In Case of Disaster

In hurricanes and floods
you can hunker down,

though you might just
blow away or drown.

In blizzards we suggest
you settle in,

with a pint of
vodka, rum or gin.

Never head up
a tree to wonder,

if some far off rumble
might be thunder.

Earthquakes will shake Ya
droughts might dry Ya,

but it is mandatory
to run from fire.

Hilde of Vienna

Hilde sits in the train station,
in a glass box built for waiting.
On a perimeter of oak slats,
She sits at first near the door.
With Her fellow travelers nearby,
a trio of blue pigeons at Her feet,
Her black valise on tiny wheels,
She is nearly ready to leave.
In a plastic bag She keeps
a warm can of beer, occasionally
tipped into a coffee cup, and
a face cloth to tidy what's near;
the prints of fingers, the lint and dust.
She withdraws a comb,
turns to the glass to face Herself,
slides it back over Her head and
again until the silver is perfect.
She continues a conversation
with a memory, while She straightens
Her plaid skirt and chases
a smudge from the tips of Her shoes.
She squeezes the pearl button
that holds the lace round Her neck.
It is a scornful glance She aims
at the ones who fail to close Her door,
rising to set it straight against the cold.
She must be off to observe a holiday,
a reunion with a child now distant,
an older sister still on the family farm,
a lover She met once on a train to Vienna.
She checks Her wrist against the station clock,
rises to go and then sits again beside Herself,
remembers to quench Her thirst and that
Her hair needs combing, the dust, Her shoes,
and of course the pearl at Her throat.

Catechism

Worship

Is the Act
Of Devoting
One's Living
To the Praising
Of all those Things
One Fears.

Faith

Is the Act
Of Throwing
Seeds into an
Ocean, believing there
Will be a Garden when
One Returns.

For Your Fourteenth Birthday
For Gregory

Over our years,
I may have
given you gifts
you were
unprepared to receive.
Blame both
your age and mine.
You so recent
in this world.
Me, old before wise
who must see you
safely on your way,
wings spread widely,
eyes upon horizons.
It might have been
simple as the sound
a bat makes
cracking a fastball,
or the smell of the air
announcing rain.
It might have been
the mystery of a Universe
forever racing from itself,
or the majesty of the notes
Beethoven set against
Schiller's Ode.
They were all offered
with an opened palm
and an earnest embrace.
All the least to be done
for bridling you with the
delicate weight of living.
But these words,
not spoken until now:
Of the miracles a man

could wish to summon,
which could make your life
sing with purpose,
I wish you someday
a son.

At the Intersection of Poetry and Road Rage

Admittedly,
the traffic was
especially fierce,
expressing into a funnel,
conforming to a bottle's throat.

The guy
with the blue kayak
tied to his roof-racks
was anxious to be paddling
over some tranquil silver estuary.

The poet
was feeling the great
terrible straining of creation,
that undefined impulse which
propels one toward beauty and truth.

He didn't
really cut her off.
There was no intended
malice from the gentle stranger
who merely hoped to share a common path.

But he
was in front now
and she held only one weapon:
the horn on which she leaned with the
entire weight of her life and she did not release it.

He performed
a dance on his brake
and she wound back and
forth like a tiger inside the
confinement of a dark cage at the zoo.

He was
unimpressed, sitting
high up over his tall wheels,
while out of her window she hurled
great declamatory passages of profanity.
And against that summer bug-strewn windshield,

she fired
the most scandalous
lines of blankest, blank verse.
Stick it up your clerihew, Pal! and
take that boat and ram it up your pantoum!
Take this villanelle straight to Dante's Hell!!!!

And he,
always the type
who was way less than impressed
by poetry and by poets, took it all
until it was all he could take and then suddenly,
without a warning, without a hint of foreshadowing

he turned left.

At the Louvre

I've been to see *The Mona Lisa*.
Traversed the angry *Atlantique*.
Dealt with Frenchmen;
Their lunging taxis.
Their coffee, dense and bitter.
Their sweet condescension.
I've stood for an hour
in a wind-driven rain.
Descended into the
great pyramid of I. M. Pei.
Paid the fare in francs
to wander that fortress
past the winged *Victory*,
the armless *Venus*,
Vermeer's *Astronomer*.
Five hundred depictions
of the dying Jesus and
the elegant portraits of
many Frenchmen who
would sadly lose their heads.
I followed the signposts,
heard my heels
down the lengths of
those long hallowed halls.
Then, at once she was there.
Her face looking back at me
over a field of cameras
held high above the crowd.
The subtle *terra incognita* of her
spattered with awe
and battery light.
And I took my turn,
slithered and gaped and
uttered *excuse moi* and
then turned my back again,
and wandered off to
the d'Orsay to
look for *Olympia*.

To Tend a Geranium

Know that they
only intend to delight,
filling a room corner
with subtle scent, then
launching their rockets
high above the crowd,
where they can burst
into balls of redness.

They demand only
that the earth stay
moist between their toes,
that you remove
the brown death from
around their shoulders.

And, like any
child of summer,
always aim them
toward the sun.

Al Qaeda Training Films, Inc.

We must begin
by loving the dust,
for it is indeed
everywhere in this world.
It made the prophet squint,
found its way into the flesh
of the most tender fruit.
It ground his teeth smooth.
And we must love
the terrible heat which
dries the dust and boils us
in our tawny flesh.
You will learn
to swing from our ladders,
somersault over limbo poles,
fire rounds from
moving motorcycles,
peer through tiny slits
from beneath black capes.
You will learn to take turns,
as you break down their doors,
take them all hostage,
commandeer their Hummers,
expose your face to fire.
But do not wonder.
All your questions will
not be answered in kind.
When it is your
turn before the camera,
hold your weapon high,
say the name of our god
over and again and
when we teach you
how to wire yourself
for the great glory,
bear the weight with humility.
For in that place where

the fruit is always clean
and the dust has settled over
all our common eternities,
be assured your reward
will be great indeed.

Poem Written Crossing the Austrian Alps

Graz to Salzburg on The Ferdinand Raimund, October 2003

Like the river,
this train
finds its
way through
the mountains
by the grace
of the low places.
Here men toil
and cows graze
beside rooftops
red with
sun and rain.
For today,
the hillsides will
speak only
oxblood and ambers,
the long valleys
still thick
with green.
Perhaps tomorrow,
the snow will
descend the slopes
and lay its
soft weight over
the months to come.

Letter to a Dying Man

It is not easy
to be the one who waits,
the one who remembers.

Those things
never fall softly
through the fingers,

landing like
a green leaf
on the grass.

Those things
are more like the pain
in a missing limb,

a photo of us
found yellowed in a box
among forgotten things.

To begin, the survivors
can never say that
this dying has its end.

The Queen of Carolina

Even when my Grandmother
was without her apron,
it was hung in plain sight.
Married sixty-two years
to a man who had her spend
the long Upstate Winters,
blanching and jarring tomatoes
he had grown from specks.
Behind the red house,
a large patch of earth he
had scarred and then fenced.
She pulled at the stones with
the teeth of a rake, to make
room for the fruits to breathe.
In his angry old age,
he would berate her while
she rinsed the greasy sauce
from his dinner plate,
concerned she was wasting soap.
Ten years have passed,
since he entered the dust.
Now, eight hundred miles
from her New York memories,
she passes the days in a place
reserved for The Elder Gentry.
Her smile is still fetching.
She is proud when they tell her
she's got a great figure
for a gal of ninety-one.
The eighty-year-old men
with their silver hair,
circle her like a warm slice
of peach pie with cream.
She loves to play cards.
Holds court around those
Big Carolina Round Tables.
Five Card Draw.

Seven Card Stud.
Even a little Night Baseball.
She looks them in the eye
and tells them all to ante up.
Beside her sink, a big old glass jar
slowly overflows with nickels.

A Former Son of the Beach

I must confess today I'm done with the beach,
Now with thousands of beach days behind me.
Lying over uncomfortable ripples of sand
Under a sun which would blister and blind me.

Oh, there were years I would long for the sea,
Sleep to the sounds of it pounding the shore.
Now it's grown too rough and too cold for me,
And as scenery it's the ultimate bore.

As a child I looked out across it with wonder,
Now I'm accused of having wound up a prig.
I contend that it was the Grand Divine Blunder,
It's obvious that the damn thing's too big.

Not to mention the various miseries endured,
From the propensities of particulate quartz.
Causing the skin and the teeth to grow more inured,
Oh, the unmentionable places it finds in one's shorts.

No, give me a porch with a lovely white railing,
A big chair for which this body was made.
Maybe a pond with a goose or two sailing,
Perhaps a couple of old trees for shade.

Stick some birds in the branches for color and song,
Bits of shadow and light for the eye.
A distance to ponder not too far or too long,
And just a hint or two of blue sky.

And you can keep the ocean and its infinite reach,
Though the multitudes with me disagree.
I've decided that I'm finally done with the beach,
Likely the beach has had it with me.

Seventeen Poets and a Potluck Dinner

It's just another
New Years Day
for the cold cut
and casserole poets.
The one-legged man
with his necklace of
popcorn and cranberries
is ready to read.

His poems are
laid out in loose leaves
like a shop manual
or a family album.
Today he is in the
Number Fourteen Slot.
He will be ready
when they call him.

Soon, the impresario will
step up to the mike
and say, "Now for
some poems from
the one-legged man
wearing a necklace of
popped corn and
cranberries."

Saturday or Sunday Morning, Early

This morning, I left our bed early.
You know how, with the early sun and silence,
my mind begins to spin like that mysterious machine
at the carnival which makes cotton candy.
I try to not disturb you, but I imagine you alone,
wandering in some storied forest with only
the lights of a big moon to suggest your steps.
Wherever you are, as our cats circle the room
stepping across clouds, I cannot be. Still,
you always tell me that you know when I am gone.

But I am never gone.

That night which folded us together has
more secrets to share with you, and I am
awake, in the company of many bushels of thoughts;
conversations I will have, poems and letters
needing to be written, and many things I placed
on my nightstand just before I shut out the light
and turned to cradle you in that rich velvet.
This morning, I am in your chair, playing out
all the many cards of my life. The air, the piano
and our cats are all still and I am listening, as I do,
for you to call out in your sleepy voice and let me know
that you have returned.

White on Rice

Sometimes I think
it would be so nice,
to be in love with
Condoleeza Rice.

I'd gaze into her eyes
and she into mine,
and we'd age gently
like a vintage wine.

She would blush at
flowers I had sent,
even show them to
the President.

We'd ignore the jeering
and all the taunts,
get great tables
at great restaurants.

At home we would
opine and quip,
she would let me
give her hair a flip.

Oh my Condee
I would say so sweet,
oh, my Dandee
she would then repeat.

Is not this life
the damnedest thing?
It's what you take
not what you bring.

I would kiss her smile
and the space between

in the back seat
of her limousine.

Like impetuous kids
we would have our fun
in the lavatory
on Air Force One.

Condoleeza, are we
not the lucky ones?
Happier than a
barrel of nuns.

In my Armani
and your Chanel suit
they'd say that couple
sure is cute.

With your security clearance
and my abject charm,
the Secret Service
would keep us from harm.

Condoleeza, your elegance
and your grace,
the way your hair
just stays in place.

And if you asked me
I would, I suppose,
go sock Ted Kennedy
in the nose.

An act of love
beyond chivalry,
your number two man
I would forever be.

The only thing which
could ever wreck us,
forced vacations down
in Crawford Texas.

But it's only sad longing
from a hopeless mush,
for your heart is a rose
in a sticker Bush.

To Begin Winter

Two squirrels
chase the last
hours of autumn
through a mantle
of brittle leaves.
A black flock
alights like snow
over the willow
beside the pond.
The sun lies
down for the night
in late afternoon.

Tonight
a warm touch
will be welcome.
A soft lamp
in a window.
A leap of flame
in the throat
of a stone hearth.
And perhaps
a single
green thought
of spring.

An Unfortunate Fluke

Lying still,
and disguised
against the
sand bay floor,
with both eyes
watching upward,
could not
spare you
from the
osprey's claw
and his
making you
his supper.
With the sun
against your
belly
white,
you make your
final
maiden
flight.

To My Young Son

There was that day in October
In a room familiar to no one,
Where your entirety rested
On less than a forearm measure.
My palm a cradle, my fingers
Expressed like new petals
Around your bud of face.

Now you like to adorn yourself
In my shirts and shoes, that
Old leather jacket you found
In the deep of my closet.
You want to stand back to back.
I feel you slide against me
As you lift your heels and
Reach to meet my shoulders.
You cast your palm on mine
And say many hopeful things.

But I tell you to sleep well,
To reach up without fearing.
The day will be upon us soon
When I will need to raise up
My face to see into your eyes,
When I will need to be
Reassured by your shoulders.
Someday I will need to
Call out to you to come close
And make of your hands
A cradle for my head.

Recalling Pipestone Minnesota, She Said …

That's what it looked like
where I was born.

Two dimensions.
The austere geometry.

The distances
intersecting at right angles.

A landscape
stricken of elevation.

Yes, there was a greening
when the June sun

lifted the corn and rye.
Yes, there were

the trickles of water
over gentle rises.

Yes, we rocked ourselves
as the prairie winds

weaved through the poplars.
But the summer died young

and when that sky
turned to slate in December,

it left a whiteness
that was deep and endless.

We burned
what we could to stay warm.

One Saturday Evening

for Louis Simpson

We are walking
along Riverside Drive,
the poet Samuel,
the woman I love, and
Liam the painter
from East 78th.
In contrast to the city,
The Drive winds
to mimic The River.
Somewhere near
95th Street, the buildings
begin to curve too.
Despite November,
a rare sun nearly remains,
the air poised and
the sense of perspiration
beneath our coats.
Against a backdrop
of diminishing light,
the trees have memory,
the last colors
are clinging to Autumn.
One of us believes
there should be a poem,
another an abstract in oil
to suggest contentment.
The woman simply
offers me her hand.
I am inclined
to agreement but
the buildings seem
filled with angels singing,
and what was left
of that daylight has
exploded over New Jersey.

I am reminded somehow,
that in a few long hours,
somewhere dark,
and also far from here,
a black sky will be weeping stars.

Middle Age

As a boy,
I fought to keep
Death behind a locked door.

Even then,
I never slept well,
remembering it was there.

Now as a man
whose children are nearly
beyond their childhoods,

I have allowed Death
to share my house,

So long as It agrees
to stay out of my way.

Memento Mori

Death has hollowed
the recesses of sight,
The Great Chamber
emptied of
dreams and dreaming.

The portals which
granted commerce
with the mortal
have been laid bare.

Are these the teeth
which ground
mammoth to morsel?

Are these hinges
the machines of
articulated thought?

Is this our truest self,
hard and smoothed,
all sharpness rounded?

Or is this bone,
resistant and resolute,
just the last
to assume the dust?

Once Home

for Annie Henry nee Kilcullen

Settled against
a trough in a hillside,
the narrow arched
doorway led southward,
backed against the sea
and shell-strewn shore.

Would it have been
your father or his who
collected and carried
each jagged stone?
Who laid them edge to
edge, corner to crenel,
until they were composed
just tall enough to contain
the height of a man?

Once a roof of crisp thatch
angled to banish
the wind and pelts of rain,
it has finally succumbed
to the vagaries of day and
the sky. Walls once sure,
downed and crumbled,
become but a simple byre
for another man's cows.

Now they and we
stand overtaken by bog iris,
fodder and new daisies.
The great struggles and small,
the turning seasons, the fiddling
and stepping long ended.

What is gone after all?
Not your name.
Not the leaning Ben Bulben.
Neither the river nor sky.
Not the serenity beside this rill.

And surely not the sea.
Not ever the ancient incessant sea.

On the Overnight from Prague

On the sofa his parents bought just fifty-four years ago,
He sits, legs folded, beside a tall window.

The tired springs which support his frame are padded over with old coats.
With the late morning sun lying across his lap,
He is on a train crossing the continent.

The changing sky is always the same.

The tenement across the way pauses along with him in the station,
Where an old woman in her window spreads and strokes the day's news.
The platform of Thompson Street fills with travelers.

The tea warms the palms which cup it.
He feels gratitude for last night's sleep.

The voice of the conductor is coming through the compartment wall.
Words in German, perhaps Dutch,
Perhaps dialect from that region near Sienna he once loved.
He knows the name of the next stop is Marseille, or Spring Street,
Barcelona or West Fourth, or
Some other somewhere along these tracks.

It matters little,
After all.
He is not disembarking.

Looking for the Uncertain Past

I wish you could have come to know my wife. You would have liked her even though she's not Irish. The young lady I was with, who I had fathered just seventeen short years ago, would have been your Great Great Grand-daughter, twice the age my Father was when you died of old age back in 1943. Finding your relatives can be trying, especially when they have been dead for so long. On the Internet (don't ask), I found your address in The 1900 Census in New York City. You and Great Grandmother were living way downtown near The Bowery at 23 Second Ave., just up from the corner of Houston. You did not yet know that she was about to conceive a son named Theodore whom she invited into the world in early 1902 who would grow up to be my Grandfather. We had pulled The Volvo (don't ask) over in front, when we heard the sirens and then all those fire trucks made the turn from Fourth Street and pinned us in good against the curb. The firemen all looked about twelve, which made me feel like an old man. The place where you had lived had become a Hess Station with a Quik Mart (don't ask) run by Pakistanis and the place where your neighbors had lived, the place where the fire seemed to be, was now The Krishna Center for Joy and Enlightenment (don't ask). The Krishnas had emerged from the front door wrapped as they are known to be in startling pastel drapes, their bald heads chilled by January and their tiny pony tails fluttering like feathers on a trout fly. The firemen rarely get flustered since 9/11 (don't ask) and just chatted it up waiting for something to happen. No one even smelled smoke. Eventually they let us drive away while they all were left to figure it out in their helmets and heavy boots. I came home later that night, opened the page of my notes about you and the rest of The Morans and marked along the margin next to 23 Second Ave. *"BUILDING NO LONGER EXISTS"*. By the way, the Brownstone at 123rd Street and Pleasant Ave. where you watched your grandchildren grow up and where the small table stood where you set your pipe and where they finally laid you out in your blue suit, well, it got bulldozed to make room for The Triboro Bridge. You'll be relieved to know that The East River is still there, but you would not want to swim in it anymore.

Light and Line and Lightness

The lamp beside my bed is faithful,
even in the dark.

The ink in my pen is smooth and blue,
and patient.

It waits for me to grasp it with hope
and draw it out across another
bare page.

This woman I have joined and who has
joined me, is cool as marble, even when
the day is hot.

She is light when the room is heavy,
an arc in a world of angles.

Tonight the lamp understands that what I need
will be the dark.

The pen knows that I have nothing at all
which needs saying.

My room is chilly sometimes even after
a warm day.

When I have become prepared to sleep,
I know that the woman will be warm,

light and lovely and

warm.

Theatre Seats

As I passed you
to assume my seat,
You had retained your face.

It was not unlike some others.

Now, aligned behind you,
you are but two shoulders
beneath a tumble of hair.
You might be my sister,
left years ago for the Midwest.
Or a lover, lost sight of
at a corner I no longer mark.
Maybe the lady on
the cross-town bus yesterday.
My Mother.
Saint Theresa.
Julia Roberts.

Even so, we are here
within the confines
of these dimmed minutes,
before an unlit stage.
For now, I am
left to wonder, before
the house goes dark,
might you turn around
just once?

What Was Once a Window

For Susannah McCorkle

You should know it
was always obvious,
that even your smiles
were uneasy. You
could seem exposed
by the sounds of your
own voice laughing.
Your nights were
never long enough.
The mornings could
offer no more
than a fleeting promise.

I remember always
how the city looked
out there beyond your
window, three hundred
paces above the street.
At times, shadows
beneath a brilliant sun.
At times, tiny lights
against a black darkness.

All of it, near and far
as dreams can seem to be.

Since I was told
that terrible news,
I have tried to make
some kind of picture
of it again and again.
The room might have
seemed warm, likely
there was at least that

small lamp left lit
on the corner table.

While all but the
night watchmen slept,
it must have been
as quiet as an hour
can become in a city
like New York City.
Somehow, where
that window is you
found a doorway, and
you stepped through it.

The Wexford Man

As a boy,
they marched you out
in foreshortened trousers,
down a lane which
cut over the lazy hills.
It was Autumn.
The air was blunt
with the balm of
the completed harvest.
The detritus of
the farmer's labors
wilted in the field
waiting for
the dying light
to carry it back
into the damp earth.
The Christian Brothers
were there beside
the creaky door, they
showed you to your seat
like a lynch mob.
To spare your soul,
they tied your left hand,
the one you favored,
to the wooden chair back.
You hammered out
their lessons
with the chosen hand,
steering the thoughts
upstream until even
your own voice failed you.
Jesus the Savior watched,
from atop the blackboard,
his tiny feet dusted with chalk,
both hands nailed
behind his back.
With your eyes upon the desk,

you offered your daily prayers
and begged forgiveness
for the one hand left free.

The Story My Grandmother Never Told Me

The days seemed so much longer then, so much to be done.
Little time for a dance or song.
Always an empty belly, the floor collecting dust.
Always one knuckle with its skin left behind on the washboard.
Still, I know we were more fortunate than most.
The widow who took in wash on the third floor.
The man who had left three fingers in the factory gears.
The old couple downstairs with the child born dull.
But hardship always paid respects.
My mother-in-law left senseless by age.
An older brother drunk again and unconscious in his chair.
My father's fiddle silent on a closet shelf.
The East Harlem cold and dark always finding an open window.
And those babies I bore who never stopped wanting.
The first-born, with his father's name, death snatched from his crib.
But it is the first little girl who I cannot forget.
The bud of her was flushed with newness, and always the hungers at night.
She drew her life from my breasts faster than I could nourish them.
She was too tiny to know my fatigue, how the mornings came so very soon.
How I protected the sanctity of her father's sleep.
I only know, I made that cradle with my arms.
I fell asleep watching her, and when I awoke
her breaths had ceased.

The Menu

I would not be the one to offer regret
If a Liver and an Onion never met,
I would not be inclined to flip my lid
Without a plate of Lox or Squid.
There are those things we will
And those things we will not eat.
What's the surprise that Sweet Breads
Are anything but sweet?
While there might be white lightning
In that Little Brown Jug
Who'd order the Escargot if the French
simply called it a Le Slug?
Head Cheese, Truffles, Sausage and Tripe,
Caviar just fish eggs with too much hype.
I'll give a pass to an Olive,
but Olive Loaf is just phony.
What a miserable way to screw up
a nice slice of Baloney.

Someday We Will All Have a Blimp

Someday,
We will all
have a blimp,
With our names
in big letters
on the sides
if we'd like.
We'll climb
into our gondolas.
Keeping our
grand nose into
the breezes, we'll
dream our dreams
to the soft hums
of our tiny propellers.
We'll count all
the swimming pools,
and scour the world
for parades and ballgames.
The sun will
make us squint,
even on cloudy days.
We'll notice
just how funny
things look from
way up there.
And maybe, one day
our beautiful wives
will come with us,
bringing along our
beautiful children.
Unless they all
awaken that morning
and decide,
it might be
a better day
to take out
the submarine.

Opus 75

For Samuel Menashe

Regret is the
great venom,
the path not
chosen finds
only the lost.

No reiteration
of moments.
No reversal
of seasons.

Just as death
lives in the
shadows left
behind, the day's
fruits will
lie wilted by
a sun which
made them sweet.

Anticipation can be
the elixir vitae.
But for certain,
there is only
this day and the
next, this day
and the next,
this day and the next.

Sparrows

If these sparrows
could only know
how perfect they are,
how venerable.

Blacks and grays,
or browns against
a top sheet of snow.
Beneath a feeder
teeming with thistle,

where goldfinches
work, clasped
to a short peg,
engaged in one more
dance with Winter.

They stab frantic
at what the finches
fail to hold, their
feet make star prints
upon the white.

Their struggle is
with the seasons,
unimpressed
with grace and
a defining silence.

On Compassion

At Darfur,
the children, weak
from emptiness,
accord the flies
the tears
from their eyes.
Neither
dares ask mercy
of the dust,
or the
kings of the world.

In Modern Times

It's seven in the morning,
or just after lunch,
or perhaps near that
time when the moon
perches atop that
old hickory in my yard.
It does not matter much,
but that I am wide awake
with this television on.
There is yet another
bulletin on the crawler,
a news alert, some
information which has
arrived from thin air.
There may be more
agents of destruction.
A bomb which has
collapsed the night
upon the sleeping.
The latest definition
of the word *jihad*.
So I feel compelled
to attend, my eyes
screwed to the news.
And I come to sleeping
slowly and jolted,
as if the wheels of my
slumber are on the rims.
For I am not fearful
of what I might
see or hear, only
what might escape me
should I stop to eat
or close both of my
eyes at one time.

On the Passing of an Old Soldier

For Bernard Ryan

It's different
when an old soldier dies.
He dies with
the memory of death.

Behind a face
he rises to meet
in the morning mirror,
a shoebox of curled,
browned images, carried
place to place, and
shown to no one.
He will shave away
the graying stubble,
prepare for a day once
seen only in a dream,
leaving the warm bed
where the mother of his
children slept beside him.

An old house filled
with the living scents
of baking and coffee
over a lingering
of last evening's fire.
A modest plot of
tomatoes and flowers
thriving in straight rows.
A place to be toiling
from the first splinters
of light to the last.

And always the
ever-deepening joys,
the places of quiet,
of cool soil and fatigue.

To Everyone's Mother

For Helene

You should know
it is not easy being
the daughter, or sister
for that matter, or
even a cousin or niece.
This life offers us
its challenges, often
with no more
than a wink.

We can take them
into our grasp or not.
No one will notice.
Ah, but to be mother,
wife, to nourish them
all, even before they are
arrived from that dream.
To caress and repair
them all, to serve
the meals warm and
fold them safe into
their sheets.

To chase the
dust and spiders,
make everything shine,
be always what
is most expected.
Those may be
the small things
used to make saints.

You should know,
I would do it all, even
if no one took account.

But you should someday.
Maybe throw a grand party
only for me, where
my guests will say
the very kindest words.
Adorn the room with flowers.
Bring me big plates
filled with favored tastes,
and sweet drinks
to make my head swim.

And someone should sing.
And someone should
ask me to dance.
And I think I will,
because you know
I deserve all of it.
But before it ends,
and you carry me home,
promise me
that someday soon,
we'll all get together
and do it again.

Dearest Terry

U.S Forest Service worker Terry Barton is charged with starting the great Hayman fire in Colorado when she set fire to a letter from her estranged husband which then got out of control. By the time of her arrest, the fire had consumed more than 130,000 acres.

Perhaps you will
think it cowardly,
this letter after
so many years
of marriage.
I could not face you.
It is not that
I don't still love you.
You know
I always will.
It was the loneliness.
The long mountain nights.
The cold side of the
bed against my back.
That unquenchable
longing for things
fondly recalled,
which now grow
ever more distant.
The memory of
your face in candlelight.
I am left behind
with the scent of pine.
Night skies
black as a broken heart.
Stars which seem
near and far
as the treetops.
I never believed I
could ever love another.
But she was so lovely
and so near and

surely you must
also feel that
our passions have lost
their fire …

Endings Shed

For Ashley

I recall how you cried
after I had cut my hair,
pointing your eyes
to the bouquet of curls
lying lifeless in a basket.
You were not even eleven.
I was not even old.
Hanging wet and heavy,
I barely coaxed the old
sewing shears through it.
I had resisted for
several long moments,
fearing the fall
to the floor below, but
it was too long, I explained,
halfway to my waist.
Five, no six years
of bramble and briar, lying
as a useless appendage
upon the long of my back.
So I consoled you, spoke
how most things must
someday be shorn or shed.
Even the taste of sweetness
can fail to linger, and
even things which do
can grow tired and wild.
You seemed to understand.
At least I believed you did.
And I still choose
to believe that now, and
that someday we may
live long enough to
never bring it to mind
again.

Beside Mozart's Grave

St. Marx Cemetery Vienna, October 2003

Consecrated with a fistful of lime,
your grave was not marked.

Your palm empty of coin,
your head eternally heavy.

They left you there young.
Beneath a modest rise of soil.

Not a crypt for princes.
Neither mount nor riverbank.

Among the broken stones.
Beside a tree with no name.

When the gravediggers found you,
at one with the cold and quiet,

it was a discarded angel
they set beside your head, her

wings in repose, eyes cast down.
Then a single pillar,

short as a stooping man,
fractured from some

forgotten temple gate.
On its flat, a gilded name

offered like a single note
to impress the afternoon's sun.

At Hard Labor

I suppose I am grateful
that writing a poem

is not like mining sulfur
from the banks of a volcano

or welding a crossbeam
miles above the street.

Nor is it like
erecting a dream house.

Most days, it is more
like splicing a phone line,

or hanging a door
on a linen closet.

After all, we live
in a world of toiling,

sweeping the dust
from the steps,

only to find them
wanting once more.

Wiping the gray mud
from our boots, then

walking out into the
field again at morning.

I have never
invited these poems, yet

they keep on arriving
one by one, shaking

the rain
from their shoulders

as they emerge from
the dark beyond my door.

I suppose I am grateful
that they did not

rob my house
or steal my children

from their
very beds.

Writing a poem
is not like

rising at first light
to cook for an army,

but more like
waking at ten on Sunday

to prepare an omelet
for someone you really love,

or teaching a small child
to lace up a shoe.

It is the dancers I pity,
who must aspire

to leap and spin, and
the painters who must

live with the burn of
turpentine in their veins.

What of the man
near the park, who stands

on the best days and the worst
turning chestnuts over tiny coals?

Or the waitress
who must always

be concerned with
what I want to drink?

Writing a poem is not
like any of that, I think.

But enough, the rain
is ferocious tonight.

So much that I fear
the hills will be washed away.

And if I am not mistaken,
there may be someone

at my door.

What Is Past Is

I am grateful
to the others
who called you
lover, wife.

Not for the
way they found
something in your
eyes when you
were both new
and looking forward.

Not for the
way their touch
had made you
rise and shudder.

Not for the
swale of the shoulders
you sought at daybreak.

And not for the
dreaming of dreams,
dreamed as one dreamer.

But only for their
coming to realize
they could not keep you.

And, of course,
for letting you go.

With Spalding on the Staten Island Ferry

In Memory of Spalding Gray

What was it in your
thoughts that Saturday
night, coursing between
the Docks of Richmond
and the Apex of Metropolis?
Above the city, you could
see all the stars and
The Towers still felled.
A headwind on
winter's coldest night
spun into your bare face
like a wheel of razors.
We can only imagine
that water to be cold.
The insistent swells.
The clots of ice.
Still you must have
felt assured, not
pausing for farewells,
a sadness like a ballast to
carry you down and down.
You must have
felt rich in that moment,
becoming finally weightless
in the pitch of that
fabled harbor, held by
that font which only
lives to feed the oceans.
We all knew where
you were going, although
we still twist to know why.
Like all those lonely souls
who traveled with you that
Saturday night, you might
just as well have headed
home.

Through a Window, Sitting

Insights condense
in the skies I test.

Figures tumble
from mist.

Yet, it is not a
bottomless blue,

which draws
my wonder.

Rather, the broad
palates of gray,

the vagaries of
the willful wind.

This Is Not a Poem about Buffalo

Yes, I've never written a poem about Buffalo,
And I think bisons are no more appealing,
Although Indians ate them and wore them as coats,
And cowboys sang about them with feeling.

You find them sprinkled over landscapes out west,
And in paintings where painters would paint them,
But if I were considering a subject to laud in verse,
I can tell you it absolutely ain't them.

They're dirty and smelly and covered with flies,
They'll stampede you with no provocation,
I'm not impressed that they're on the nickel's back,
To me they're just bulls with a bad reputation.

So don't look for any poem from me,
About these beasts with a hump and goatee,
An ode to an eagle or perhaps a horse,
But never an ode to a buffalo from me.

One Reflection

Tonight, I captured you
in the passive reflections
of a grand window,
its glass blackened by
the eager December dark.

Lighting two candles,
held with upright dignity
by columns of crystal.
The falling trails of last
evening's flicker, a history.

I heard in the air,
the soft jostle of matchsticks
from the tiny paper box
we collected one
brilliant day in Paris.

The scent of your efforts
rose and flowed into the
distant corners of the room.
Soon there should be wine,
the taste of a thousand hands.

You will look across the
table at me, in that way,
your eyes reminding how
the tree of contentment
must be established
in gratitude.

Beatrice

She might have been
The Gibson Girl, or
that model in an ad
for fine silk stockings.
A lady with a grand
feathered felt hat.
Her back stood straight.
Her head was fitted
with a crown of curls,
brown eyes emitting light.

Near an end which came
over her too slowly,
her body leaned over
a cane which resisted
the weight of her
for as long as it could.
She wore wool for warmth.
Her hair, gray wisps
held back by simple clips.
Her eyes had been dimmed
like a theatre on Sunday.

Still she never ventured
out without lipstick,
deep red to match
her fingernails.
She would apologize
for not looking her best,
for taking so desperately
long to cross the room.

I would always tell her
she looked just fine,
and not to hurry and
let's agree to
continue believing that

youth and beauty
are the twin illusions.
We have nothing if not time.

After Martin Tucker's *The Missing Father*

Unlike you, I cannot
write about a father
who left when I was
just a small boy.

There was no shouting in
the kitchen at midnight.

There was never an
empty bottle in the morning.

Never the scent of
foreign things trapped
in his clothing.

He walked through his door
each night, at just before six.

He loved Jesus and
General Motors and
Barry Goldwater as well.

The suits in his closet stood
as gray and brown soldiers,
prepared for the great
battles of midtown.

Still, there was rarely
the evening when I
would not be watching him,
when I could feel assured
of his breathing.

There was never the day
when I was not swallowed
by his silence and by waiting.

In those green days and these,
my mother would say to me,
Your father loves you, you know.

But as a child and as a man
I said that I understood
some things which I did not.

How could one be certain
of things such as that?
How many words were invented,
in how many languages,
by how many people in this life?

He could not chose even one
that he could live with.

For most of my life,
I have been disturbed
by silence the way some
people are disturbed by
storms or windy nights.

It has been forty-seven
years and now I have
just this single request:

Allow me what remains of my life
to forget all those things
I cannot remember.

Another Sunset

You know how
it is with sunsets.

Especially ones over water.

There is always
the fiery orb, dropping
painfully, delightfully slow.

That characteristic shimmering.

The clouds, illuminated
from the bottom up.
The revealing of color

which begins with
a brilliant orange,
then melts into reds and

cools and cools
into purples and blues.

Usually you find
yourself startled at the
sudden fact of darkness,

as if you had just awakened
from an unplanned snooze.

You find
the definition of the world
is going, and sense

that the eyelids of
everything are growing heavy.

A Midtown Christmas

Across West 57th Street
the wind is cutting,
cold enough to drive
the rich ladies into
their leathers and ermine.
Along Columbus Circle
ten dollar pashminas are
flying off folding tables.
In this warm café
across from Carnegie Hall,
the water is clear,
the coffee a black aroma.

It is only another
last Saturday before
another Christmas and
the ghost of my self
looks back inside
from a wall of glass.
The Pakistani's sunglasses
are frozen on a pegboard.
The tourists from
Dayton and Wichita
crane their necks and try
to locate the top of the sky.

In a few days we will
consider the doors
to be opened and closed.
Inhale the airs
let into a stuffy room.
In a few days it will all
be wrapped and unwrapped.
Another set of memories
added to the ones we never had.

A Greeting to Friends

My wife is one of
those rare people who
insist on greeting
the creatures she encounters.
The wary deer on our lawn.
The goldfinches
arranged like grapes
on the feeder.
The elegant red fox
who appears like
a phantasm and goes.
The Great Blue Heron
at the pond's edge
is her friend, as is
the neighbor's kitten
and the old hound dog
who visits often.
Even the white moth
who slipped in
the kitchen door is
addressed with high regard,
caught in an old water glass
and set free. But when
an ant or wasp cannot
be dissuaded she
will ask their forgiveness
and bless them saying,
Be with Buddha,
and only then
will she dispatch them
with a good swat,
to the hereafter.

The Swimming Lesson

Down at the tired shores
of Florence Avenue Beach,
an optimist in green trunks
was instructing us on
how to become swimmers.

We, a dozen or so
scrawny specimens on
an early summer day.
One o'clock sharp,
up to our tiny thighs
in that oily chill.

We knew there
were secrets, that things
lived beneath it all.
We knew, as we stood,
within minutes
the sandy bottom
would swallow our feet.
Our young mothers
looked on from old blankets,
proud for unknown reasons.

Then the instructor said,
with great authority,
First thing we'll learn
is the dead man's float.
Some cried, but most tried
facing down
into the briny darkness.
We let the bubbles rise
back across our cheeks.

And we made believe
we had failed
to learn to swim.

For Liam Roberts

*No artist can paint what he sees. The world can never quite
look like a picture, but a picture can look like the world.*

— Ernst Gombrich

Within this
hidden corner of living,
the walls are near,
the ceiling becomes
a crumbling geography
you wander in twilight.
The breaths you've drawn,
collected and counted,
stowed well into
black boxes and shelved.
Your room overflows
its bounds with light.

You showed it all,
the many days and nights
resurrected from a pallet
thick as a headstone.
Arranged now, scattered
onto every horizontal.
Hundreds at least.
Each in procession
more splendid.
Your colors speaking.
A pale glowing
at the edges of shade.

You said,
look carefully
behind and beyond
this mad geometry.
Here is
an animal I
constructed from

a random thought.
There's a figure
of a woman, a man.
Here is a head,
a face.

One Moment along a Street in Kensington

Behind window glass,
cut into a recess of brick,
and four floors over the street,
the lady of the house is standing,
her ample waist pressed
to the basin rim.

A black car passes
below, then another.
All is damp with the sheen
of an early morning rainfall.

A young mother
forces her pram down
toward a familiar corner.

In a doorway
a wisp of a man
expresses smoke up
into the heavy air.

Rain clouds
withhold and somersault
over the rooftops.

Behind the window
the lady guides water
over a breakfast dish,
lays down the rag
to scratch at
a reluctant speck
of clotted egg.

Content, she places it
into a wooden rack.
She takes up
what is next,

a teacup,
her husband's fork.

The water
collects and falls
toward a dark place.

The man
casts his fag end
into the gutter.

The taxi is lost
along the distance
as is the next.

The lady of the house
disappears into
the silent inner elsewhere,
as the last of the moisture
runs from the plates,

as the young mother
turns her pram
at the corner and
is gone.

To the Woman at the Party Last Night
Who Just Had to Bring It Up

Don't think that I don't get your point.
Even if it makes no sense at all,
it was still well articulated.
Perhaps it was how you offered it.
Like a platter of delicate tastes
with a bit too much curry.
If I try, I can see things your way.
You know I want to, but
it feels like I'm forcing my foot
into a shoe which is ill-fitted.
Like sleeping in someone else's bed.
After all, we are all humans,
each of our skulls slightly misshapen,
and filled with such separate thoughts,
each of us fighting back the overgrowth
along the course of our chosen path.
But please, consider re-thinking it all
and I pledge to do the same.
We can agree that it's only fair, then
having given both opinions fair chance,
at least one of us will be certain,
that you were completely wrong.

Ka-Ching

At the Indian
Casino, the Redmen
are caste in bronze.
The pale faces
put on their
dress sweatshirts
and sneakers,
strap on a
fanny pack full
of the rent.

Pinching tax-free
cigarettes and a
bucket of silver,
they wander
wide-eyed and
press their luck
with the gods of
buzzers and bells,
spinning cherries,
reluctant sevens.

Here on
the reservation,
the buses are
regular and free,
the burgers cheap
and lukewarm,
and all the hours
become lost in
the ethers of chance.

August Mosca Is Dead

8 January 2003

The day you died,
it snowed.

Not the
kind of snow
to make mothers
run for
milk and eggs.

Not the
kind of snow
which weighs
down the long
boughs of trees.

Not the
kind of snow
which stings
the face and hands.

It was an
unexpected snow.

One which fell
through the
last moments
of a January night,
on the supine
breath of
an arctic front.

The kind of snow
which falls
in dreams.

The kind of snow
you would have
marveled at as
you laid the
first brushfull of
Titanium white
on a blank canvas.

On Descent

I know your name.
The day you were born and where.
My Grandfather's
Grandfather's Grandfather.
And I know many things
about your world, which
you could not have known.
The wars ahead, the lighting
of darkness, and millions
of miracles and small tragedies.
I know about people
that you never got to know
and what happened
to them all in the end.

For you, the past
was no more or less than
the present or the future.
There was only time
for work and for rest and
for worrying about
keeping the rain on the field,
the cold on the far side of the door,
and a God in his heaven.

No one has survived who knew you.
No one to say a kind word
or a bitter one.
No one but I, has even spoken
your name out loud in
a very long hundred years.
The days will always exceed us.

My desire has made you a face,
made your voice reassuring as it
praised a fair day or a warm meal.
I have made you the man

you should have been.
There is little of the truth
in any of it, but a grandfather
should be who you need him to be.
Perhaps such are the desires of a fool.

Still, one certain thing will not be ignored.
The debt which cannot be settled, and
how many things finally came
from but a single moment
in the arms of the woman you took as yours.

In Response

I wish that
you had not
given me that
poem to read.
I tried my best
to perch it
on my fingers,
to examine it
with due care,
with tenderness
and expectation.

You thought
too highly of it.

Like any confection,
too delicate,
too sweet,
even under
the gentle pressure
and the warmth
of my hold,
it had become,
within moments,
a gooey mess.

Note to a Soldier

It is my
April morning,
against a hill
unacquainted with turmoil.

My hands
are drawn around
this warm cup.
This woman

who loves me,
is near enough
to hear my breathing.
Yet, in all this

I am conscious
of you, huddled
into dark ditches,
holding lightly to

a rifle and
a dream of sleep.
Slow, the grieving
falls through me.

Deep,
within my ribs,
my heart
tastes its dying.

Some Instructions

When my time comes.
Don't lay me in a box
with long bronze handles.
Don't comb my hair
the way you always
thought it should go
and lay my head on satin.
Don't polish my shoes.
or surround me
with grand bouquets.
Flowers die too soon.
Don't embrace one another
or blot the grief
from your eyes.
I will not have it.
There should be
no coffee, no cakes.
No one sing Amazing Grace.
And please, no churches,
no suggestions of the
mysterious will of
a god I deny.
I am not going home and
I will not rest in peace.
There can be no
peace in extinction.
Be certain that
I did not go willingly. Yet,
forego your misgivings.
Act as you will, as you must.
I will not raise up
a single objection, only
be sure to have someone
say that given the chance,

I would have stayed a bit longer.